Walther Ziegler

Sartre
in 60 Minutes

Translated by
Alexander Reynolds

My thanks go to Rudolf Aichner for his tireless critical editing; Silke Ruthenberg for the fine graphics; Lydia Pointvogl, Eva Amberger, Christiane Hüttner, and Dr. Martin Engler for their excellent work as manuscript readers and sub-editors; Prof. Guntram Knapp, who first inspired me with enthusiasm for philosophy; and Angela Schumitz, who handled in the most professional manner, as chief editorial reader, the production of both the German and the English editions of this series of books.

My special thanks go to my translator

Dr Alexander Reynolds.

Himself a philosopher, he not only translated the original German text into English with great care and precision but also, in passages where this was required in order to ensure clear understanding, supplemented this text with certain formulations adapted specifically to the needs of English-language readers.

Bibliographic Information held by the German National Library: The details of the original German edition of this publication are held by the German National Library as part of the German National Bibliography; detailed bibliographical data can be found online at www.dnb.de.

© 2016 Dr Walther Ziegler
1st Edition June 2016
Jacket design and graphic design for the whole book: Silke Ruthenberg, making use of illustrations by:
Raphael Bräsecke, Creactive – Studio for Advertising, Comics & Illustrations
© JackF - Fotolia.com (image-frames)
© Valerie Potapova - Fotolia.com (image-frames)
© Svetlana Gryankina - Fotolia.com (speech-balloons)

Publisher and Printing:
BoD – Books on Demand, Norderstedt
ISBN 9783741227721

Contents

Sartre's Great Discovery — 7

Sartre's Central Idea — 14

    Man is Condemned to be Free — 14

    Freedom and Guilt — 18

    Freedom as 'Ek-stasis' or 'Standing-Out' — 23

    The 'For-Itself' and the 'In-Itself' — 29

    The Three 'Ek-stases' of Temporality — 32

    "Bad Faith" ("Mauvaise Foi") — 39

    Nothingness — 44

    'Looking' and 'Being-Looked-At' — 51

    Shame Under the "Look of the Other" — 57

    "Being-For-Others" as Struggle for Recognition — 64

    Love as the Surmounting of Struggle? — 68

    Absolute Freedom and Absolute Responsibility — 76

Of What Use Is Sartre's Discovery for Us Today? — 80

    Leave "Bad Faith" Behind – Go Your Own Way — 80

    Don't Just Dream – Put Your Thoughts and Ideas into Practice — 85

If Necessary, Be Ready to Rethink	89
Become Political – The Courage to Intervene	93
Bibliographical References:	**99**

Sartre's Great Discovery

The French existentialist Jean-Paul Sartre (1905-1980) is one of the most important philosophers of the 20th Century. He became world-famous through his provocative thesis that Man is 'condemned to be free'. His existentialist demand that, in the face of the certainty of death, we cease to believe in some heavenly 'beyond' and form our lives freely and determinedly in the here and now became the credo of a whole generation:

Man is nothing other than what he makes of himself. This is the first principle of existentialism. [2]

Sartre's philosophy of existence did not only influence academic discussion at universities; it exerted its effect on the whole of Western civilization, above all on European youth.

Existentialism became a kind of lifestyle: high-school pupils, students and artists, along with other enthusiasts for this worldview, began to meet regularly in cafés. This, admittedly, was nothing new in France. But these open discussion-circles, shared in equally by men and women, gave rise to a youth culture of their own. As a sign of their shared existentialist attitudes, participants wore dark clothing and horn-rimmed glasses, following Sartre himself. The existentialists' motto ran: Do not let anyone tell you how you must live; decide yourself how to act and stand by the things you do; live earnestly and intensively both in your love affairs and friendships and in your political commitments.

Sartre himself strongly emphasized this last point: that existentialism is not just a call to individual self-realization but, above and beyond this, also a call to social commitment:

And when we say that Man is responsible for himself, we do not mean that he is responsible only for his own individuality, but that he is responsible for all men. [3]

This led existentialists to demonstrate both against French colonial wars in Algeria and Indochina and against American imperialism in Vietnam. Their rejection of bourgeois morality also prompted them to experiment with free love. Sartre himself maintained an 'open relationship' with his lifelong companion Simone de Beauvoir. That is to say, both partners sometimes entered into intimate relations with others – which never, indeed, endangered their deep attachment to one another. They even concluded a 'contract of freedom and openness', in which they declared their rejection of bourgeois conventions of monogamy while at the same time committing themselves to always remaining honest with, and therefore, to one another.

Besides his philosophical books, Sartre also wrote many novels and plays. But above all he showed active political engagement, organizing countless petitions and, after four years' support of the Communist Party, subscribing to moderate forms of Maoist political positions. When, in 1957, he threw his support behind Algerian independence and urged French soldiers to refuse to fight in Algeria, his apartment was completely destroyed in a bomb attack mounted by angry conservative-nationalist forces.

He also sought dialogue, all his life, with revolutionaries and social outsiders, visiting Che Guevara, Fidel Castro, Mao Zedong and – when he was already over seventy – the imprisoned members of the Baader-Meinhof gang. During this latter prison visit he lodged a strong protest, despite his age and failing eyesight, against the isolation in which Baader and the others were held.

Like many of his existentialist contemporaries, Sartre was a heavy smoker. Still today the menu of his favourite Paris café, the Café de Flore, includes an 'existentialist breakfast' priced at only two euros. It seems a good price – until one sees that it consists only of a cup of black coffee and an unfiltered cigarette. But just such 'purism' – the decision to breakfast on just that which mattered to the individual without all the 'bourgeois' trappings – really was part of the existentialist attitude to life. It was in the same spirit that Sartre refused to accept the Nobel Prize for Literature, which seemed to him to be mere 'bourgeois' pomp.

All aspiration toward security, comfort and acquisition of possessions seemed contemptible to the existentialists: a sign one was not truly free. Sartre was consistent here and lived his whole life in bare hotel rooms. It was also important to him that he composed all his literary and philosophical works at

Sartre's Great Discovery

tables that were not his own.

He was, however, a little disturbed by the youth culture that adopted him as its figurehead, fearing that he would no longer be taken seriously by scholars. But his fears proved ungrounded. His principal work, which appeared in 1943 with the provocative title *Being and Nothingness*, still counts as a milestone in the history of philosophy. In this book Sartre declares freedom to be the decisive core of Man. No other philosopher before or since has accorded such tremendous significance to human freedom of decision.

> Freedom is total and infinite [...]. The only limits which freedom bumps up against [...] are those which it imposes on itself. [4]

Still today, Sartre is considered to be *the* philosopher of freedom. But this is not all. He also made a second discovery of great consequence. He was one of the first philosophers to investigate the structure of inter-human relations. Among the phenomena he analysed here was love – and he arrived at an astonishing insight: each human being, if he is to develop any sort of sense or idea of himself, is existentially dependent upon the love, the opinion, and the reactions of other human beings. Sartre, indeed, sees freely-accorded recognition by our fellow human beings as forming the very basis of our being. On the other hand, though, we experience just this constant exposure to being judged by others (or, as Sartre prefers to phrase it, by 'the Other') as something threatening, because beyond our control:

> We have observed that the Other's freedom is the foundation of my being. But precisely because I exist by means of the Other's freedom, I have no security. I am in danger in this freedom. [5]

This danger – which Sartre calls 'ontological' – consists in the fact that we do indeed desire to be recognized by others but can never be sure of this recognition because 'the Other' is, in principle, free and can always reject and refuse to recognize us. Even a love relationship, in which the lovers offer unconditional mutual recognition to one another, can suffer a crisis or a split. We are involved, therefore, says Sartre, in a ceaseless 'struggle for recognition'. Since this struggle belongs to the very structure of what it is to be human, Sartre draws here the provocative conclusion:

Conflict is the original meaning of being-for-others. [6]

But this insight gives rise to a whole series of questions. Is there really, for humankind, no way out of the 'struggle for recognition'? Might a solution to this conflict not be found in love? Why does Sartre believe that love is bound to fail? And above all: what becomes of our freedom if we are constantly dependent on assurance derived from others? Is there really such a thing as 'freedom' at all?

Sartre's Central Idea

Man is Condemned to be Free

Man, claims Sartre, is not just free in his decisions; he is 'condemned to be free'. Neither inherited dispositions nor education can limit Man's freedom. He is *absolutely* free and must, therefore, in every moment consider what to do – and what not to. This structure is inherent in Man's very essence. It is not that a human being enters the world and only subsequently wins freedom; rather, he is born free:

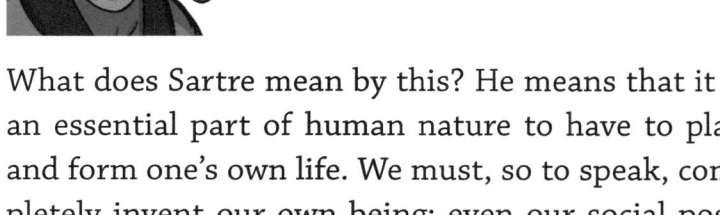

Man does not exist *first* in order to be free *subsequently*; there is no difference between the being of Man and his *being-free*. [7]

What does Sartre mean by this? He means that it is an essential part of human nature to have to plan and form one's own life. We must, so to speak, completely invent our own being: even our social position, our character and our body.

Sartre's Central Idea

Sartre knows, of course, that no one can decide whether he is born rich or poor. He also knows that there exist genetic predispositions over which we have no control, such as the colour of our eyes or hair and how tall or muscular we are. He himself, for example, was barely five foot tall, so was certainly aware that we are all born with strengths and weaknesses that we did not choose. Nevertheless, he insisted that even such innate traits of character and physique do not prevent us from being absolutely free.

We always have the opportunity to take up a stance, and to behave in a certain way, vis-à-vis these innate traits and qualities. One is free, for example, to find one's eye-colour, physique, or particular gifts either beautiful or ugly, good or bad. And one can freely decide whether to treat one's small stature either as an excuse for leading an unhappy life or, on the contrary, as a spur to achieve great things.

> Man is nothing other than his own project. He exists only to the extent that he realizes himself. [8]

15

This means that our lives have, in their very essence, something provisional and incomplete about them. Each second, we 'plan ourselves' anew and decide which direction we want to develop in. But what of our upbringing, our background, and our early experiences? Are we not informed by our own past? Are many paths of development not closed to us early on, for example through not having received proper education? Sartre's answer here is a clear 'no'. An unhappy childhood can be treated either as a reason to hang oneself or, on the contrary, as a spur to making one's adult life especially happy and successful. Sartre, then, puts no faith in that pedagogical theory whereby upbringing and early childhood experiences leave their mark on the human being and his character as if he were malleable clay. Nor is Sartre willing to grant decisive importance to the 'drives' and 'traumas' which the psychoanalyst Freud believed he had discovered in Man:

> On the contrary, [...] (we) reject [...] equally the theory of malleable clay and that of the bundle of drives [...]. [9]

Our freedom, then, according to Sartre, is always absolute. This, however, is not just a gift; it is also a burden. Since we are free, we must constantly be deciding whether and what we want. We cannot simply let ourselves be carried along by life but must rather actively form and shape it. And for Sartre this really is a case of '*must*'. Man really has no choice but to do this:

> Man is condemned to be free: condemned, because he did not create himself, yet nonetheless free, because once cast into the world, he is responsible for everything he does. [10]

Since no one asks us beforehand whether we wish to come into the world as a stone, a flower or a human being, we are 'condemned' to live with our human freedom of decision.

Freedom and Guilt

Here we have already arrived at Sartre's central idea. Since Man is in fact free and is compelled to choose, he necessarily makes himself guilty. It doesn't matter whether the choice that is made is a good or a bad one; Man makes himself guilty in any case. Grasping certain possibilities always means rejecting certain others:

Every choice, as we shall see, supposes elimination and selection. [11]

If I study philosophy, I can no longer become an astronaut or a doctor; if I marry, I can no longer be single. Thus, a groom, before the altar, swears to always be faithful to his chosen bride and to forgo all other lovers. This sad farewell to the possibility of other choices is marked, in many cultures, by a 'stag night' on which the groom enjoys his freedom one last time and all is permitted him before he 'forsakes all others' for his bride's sake. But such a process of leave-taking does not occur only in the case of such big decisions as choosing a spouse or a profession but rather many times daily in a hundred more trivial situations. It is the sum of all these big and small decisions that determines the course of one's life. By, for example, reading this book about Sartre and learning about existentialism, you are also making a choice. You are choosing not to spend time with friends or go to the cinema. Every decision, then, is a selection. But what if one refuses to make any choice at all? Sartre discussed also this possibility:

We can choose ourselves as fleeing, as inapprehensible, as indecisive etc. We can even choose not to choose ourselves. [12]

Once can, then, choose not to choose – but in doing so, one has still made, even without wanting to, a choice. If I decide not to begin a new relationship or a new job because I can't or won't make a choice,

I have thereby made a decision after all, namely, the decision to continue with the same life I've led up till now. And I have to answer for this, just as I would have to answer for some new end I might have set myself:

The responsibility for these ends falls on us. Whatever our being may be, it is a choice. [13]

Because we bear full responsibility for our ends we become guilty. What Sartre calls 'guilt' here is not moral guilt, like, for example, the guilt incurred by breaking one of the Ten Commandments or breaking a law. Nor is it guilt vis-à-vis God or our fellow men. Initially, it is guilt vis-à-vis ourselves. Because by our decision for a particular job, partner, or country to live in, it is *ourselves* that we have robbed of many other possibilities. This kind of guilt – in other words, responsibility – is, argues Sartre, unavoidable:

Sartre's Central Idea

> Man [...] cannot avoid choosing. He will choose to abstain from sex, or to marry without having children, or marry and have children. Whatever he does, he cannot avoid bearing full responsibility for his situation. [14]

Our freedom 'condemns' us, then, to absolute responsibility. But this 'condemnation' has its positive side. Choice, and the elimination of unchosen possibilities, gives to every moment – or, as Sartre prefers to put it, every 'situation' – its special significance. Being mortal, we cannot re-choose our choices as often as we wish. If we lived forever, it would indeed be possible to practice, one after the other, all imaginable professions, learn all musical instruments, train ourselves to perfection in all sports, and engage in an infinite number of love affairs. Everything would be arbitrary, since we would always be able to choose, at some later point, what we had initially chosen to forgo. But since death awaits all human beings at some not-so-distant point, each moment of our lives is in fact unique and unrepeatable. There are many choices that one will only have one chance in one's life to make. Even the smallest life-decisions, however, inevitably involve us in that 'responsibility vis-à-vis our own existence' of which we have spoken.

The central idea of Sartre's philosophy is now clearer: Our freedom is a threefold 'condemnation'. Firstly, we are 'thrown' into existence, without being asked, as free beings; secondly, we must constantly, day by day, choose certain possibilities and forgo others; and thirdly, we are condemned to take responsibility for this choosing and forgoing and to take upon ourselves the 'guilt' implied by it.

Freedom as 'Ek-stasis' or 'Standing-Out'

It is also human freedom that forms the basis for the possibility of *failing* – something which, Sartre argues, a stone, say, or a plant can never do. Because a stone does not *exist* – or at least not in Sartre's emphatic sense of 'existence'. The stone is merely 'there'. It makes no decisions. What Sartre calls 'existence' is a certain 'standing out' into a realm of freedom in which a stone can have no part. Sartre draws here on the Latin root of our modern word 'exist': *'ex-istere'*, implying 'stand out' or 'go forth'. Man, as Sartre puts it, 'hangs suspended' in his own freedom because this freedom causes him to 'jut out' beyond the mere 'there-ness' of his physical body into a transcendental sphere:

[...] The essence of the human being is suspended in his freedom. [15]

What does Sartre mean by this? Man is 'suspended' in his own freedom inasmuch as he must adopt an observer's standpoint outside of his own self, thus becoming an object to himself. In contrast to the stone or the plant, Man is a being catapulted out of the context of Nature – a 'freedman' vis-à-vis Nature's rigid, unfree order who, as such, needs still to create and 'choose' his own self:

Man makes himself; he does not come into the world fully made. [16]

This is a quality which, Sartre argues, is exclusive to Man. A tick, for example, is firmly bound into a mechanism of stimulus and response. It knows no such 'standing out' from Nature as Sartre refers to when he speaks of 'existence' as an '*ek-stasis*'. The tick is, as the famous naturalist Jakob von Üexküll once put it, perfectly interwoven with the natural order in a fixed functional plan. Its perception of the world is narrowly limited. It has a perception of altitude sufficient to allow it to take its place on a branch and a much more developed perception for the sweat of living bodies in the form of butyric acid and heat. It has, however, neither sight nor hearing. A tick may wait on its branch for several months, without nourishment, before a deer happens by. When one does, the tick senses already from far away how the smell of sweat grows stronger and stronger until it finally reaches such an intensity that the tick drops from its branch and clings to the deer. But this dropping from the branch is not a choice, not an existential decision, in Sartre's sense. It is, of course, very important, indeed a matter of life and death, for the tick that it drops at exactly the right moment. If it drops a minute too soon or too late it may have missed its only chance. But still its action is, for the tick, completely unproblematical. No tension or nervousness attaches to this action because the tick does not have to, indeed *cannot*, make a 'decision' in Sartre's sense. It is compelled to drop from its branch at just that moment at which the smell of sweat attains a certain empirically measurable intensity. And even if a sudden gust of wind happens to come and make the tick miss its landing on the deer, the tick will feel no regret or remorse, because it never becomes an object to itself. It possesses, as Sartre would put it, no 'transcendence'. 'Transcendence' comes from the

Latin word *'transcendere'* and means to 'rise beyond'. The tick, then, possesses no capacity to 'rise beyond' Nature but is rather firmly fixed within Nature's design. It is itself part of objective Nature. Or, as Sartre says, it is a mere "in-itself", something which just "is what it is". Man, on the other hand, needs to "project himself into the future" and therefore always exists also (in Sartre's phrase) as a "for-itself". Man's essence is not defined but is rather always yet-to-be-defined. This is why Sartre can say:

[...] Man [is] a being in whom existence precedes essence. [17]

This often-quoted sentence is particularly important when read in the context of the history of philosophy. Sartre is, in fact, criticizing here the whole Western tradition of philosophical 'essentialism'. Because all philosophers prior to him, from Plato through Augustine up to Schelling, had propounded rather the opposite thesis: namely, that there are so-called 'essences' – timeless ideas and eternal entities – which precede individual human existence. The Greek philosopher Plato, for example, had contended that the essential 'Ideas' of the Good, the True and the Beautiful, which he also called the 'Idea of Justice', were of divine nature and thereby completely independent of the concrete human individual. Human beings are born and, at some point, die; but the 'Idea' of Goodness or Justice is eternal. All that individual human beings can do, says Plato, is strive to 'participate', during their mortal existences, in this eternal 'Idea', taking it as their guide and compass. Only in this way, Plato argues, can Man live 'essentially'. But to make one's existence a 'participation' in something is to accept this thing's precedence vis-à-vis one's existence. For Plato, essence precedes existence.

Sartre vehemently denies this claim of Plato's and argues exactly the opposite: no idea, no conception of justice, indeed no idea at all, can possibly arise or take form except in and by concretely existing human beings. Before anything else, there must exist a concrete human being who forms thoughts and who 'projects' himself and his world. Sartre clarifies the complex meaning of this 'projection' – which combines the idea of someone's 'throwing himself forward' into the future and the idea of his making this future a conscious personal 'project' or plan – in the following passage:

Man is, before all else, something that projects itself into a future and is conscious of doing so [...]. Prior to that projection of the self, nothing exists, not even in divine intelligence, and Man shall attain existence only when he is what he projects himself to be. [18]

This is why, in Sartre's philosophy, existence – i.e. the living human being – precedes essence.

The 'For-Itself' and the 'In-Itself'

Sartre took over the concepts 'for-itself' and 'in-itself' from Hegel and uses them throughout the length of his principal philosophical work *Being and Nothingness*. What they describe is basically something quite simple.

Sartre calls Man the 'for-itself' because Man is the only being that can develop an 'outside view' upon itself and thereby an opinion of itself. Only Man can call himself to account for his decisions, regret them, be proud or ashamed or regretful of them. A stone or a plant, by contrast, is only what it is *in itself* (never *for itself*). In Sartre's philosophy, indeed, the concepts 'Man', 'freedom' and 'for-itself' function more or less as synonyms. He uses sometimes one of these terms, sometimes another, but he basically means the same thing by all of them. It is always a matter of the human being's having to take charge *of himself*, plan and project the future *for himself*, and bear responsibility *for himself* and his actions. And it is with this actually very simple notion that Sartre explains, in a provocative manner, the essential nature of human freedom:

> We shall see [...] that the being of for-itself is defined as being what it is not and not being what it is. [19]

To have understood this sentence is to have understood the core of Sartre's whole philosophy of human existence. At first sight, indeed, the sentence is confusing and contradictory. But this puzzling statement: "the being of *for-itself* is defined as being what it is not and not being what it is" proves really to convey an important idea. If, while reading this book on Sartre, you fold the corner of a page over to mark the point you've read to, this doesn't matter to the book, since it feels no pain. Indeed, even to say that it 'doesn't matter' to the book is to say too much, since the book is not even aware of what is done to it. It is, as Sartre says, a pure 'in-itself' which is what it is and no more. Human existence, by contrast, is never only "that which it is" at any given moment. Being a 'for-itself', it can never be entirely comprised and submerged within whatever constitutes it here and now.

Even if someone pinches his finger in something, he is never completely submerged in his pain; even as he feels it, he makes himself an object of observation for himself and begins in a split second to consider what kind of new 'project' or 'self-projection' he must engage in in order to deal effectively with the pain. This is why the being of the human individual never consists only in that which he is at any given moment but always already a little in that which he is going to be in future. The human 'for-itself' can, at any second, make itself into something new, or at least conceive the plan to no longer be that which it (presently) is. And this is the first step to understanding the sentence just quoted: "Man is defined as being what he (as yet) is not and not being what he (presently still) is". Man, in other words, is always 'a step ahead of himself'. The facts of the matter here are explained to us in an especially striking way by Sartre in his remarks on time and temporality.

The Three 'Ek-stases' of Temporality

Sartre distinguishes between three different perceptions of time, the so-called 'temporal *ekstases*': past, present, and future. Sartre once again uses the term *ek-stasis* in its etymological Greek sense here, since we human beings 'jut out', in every moment of our existence, not only into the present dimension but also into the dimensions of past and future. Once again, it is the notion of freedom that is decisive here. We are, Sartre claims, free vis-à-vis all three temporal *ekstases*: future, present and past. Freedom vis-à-vis the future is an easy notion to grasp. It means simply that we can always form new future-related 'projects' and thus 'project ourselves' into the future. I can, for example, if I am unsatisfied with my current job, retrain and try in this way, to realize, say, the dream of being, instead of a bookkeeper, a tour guide who works in exotic lands. Clearly, then, I am free vis-à-vis the future.

It is also clear that I can affect, through my powers of free decision, the present, namely, by spontaneously moulding and changing it. But what about the past? Surely there can be no freedom vis-à-vis the past, since the past is what is done and finished with and no one can change what has happened in his life once it has happened. One may indeed *wish* that one's past had been better than it was – but one's past will stay one's past for all one's present wishes. How, then, can Sartre seriously maintain that we enjoy freedom even vis-à-vis our past?

He maintains this by arguing that the significance of 'the future' is by no means confined *solely* to the realm of what we will do, or want to do, *in* the future. Rather, the temporal *ekstasis* 'future' contributes to the making of Man's present and past as well, inasmuch as my freedom to make plans, to choose, to decide, always has an effect on my experience not just of my present but even of my past. For example, if I plan to stop, one day, being a bookkeeper and become an architect, I may well take up the study of architecture part-time – and this future-related project will already alter the quality of my present, making it easier, perhaps, for me to bear the tedious bookkeeping job, since I can now look on it merely as a bridge to a new and more satisfying professional challenge.

In this light one can grasp the deeper meaning of this apparently so illogical proposition of Sartre's that 'the for-itself is defined as being what it is not and not being what it is'. The fact is that Man is indeed not only that which he was, or is in the present moment, but is rather always, to some extent, that which he *not (yet)* is but has formed the project of being in future. The bookkeeper who is studying to be an architect is no longer *only* a bookkeeper even if he was one for a long time. He is already, just a little, an architect, even if he is not yet actually one. This is the way that the future alters the quality of the present. But Sartre argues more than this: namely, that Man's 'projection' of his being into the future can alter the quality of the past as well:

I alone, in fact, can decide at each moment the *bearing* of the past; [...] by projecting myself toward my ends, I preserve the past with me, and by action I decide its meaning. [20]

The past, indeed, is a 'given' and, as a 'given', not to be reversed. But through our (as Sartre says) 'projection of ourselves toward our ends' we can change the *meaning* that we give to the past. Each new 'projection' in this sense is a new orientation and each new orientation disturbs the continuity in which all past events had stood. Like the pearls in a necklace whose string has been broken, these past events roll into confusion and are then 're-strung' in a manner oriented to and by the new 'project' that I have formed.

In our example, the future architect comes to experience his own past in a different way. He may have been told as a child that he was dull and simple for spending hours playing with building blocks and taking no interest in anything else – and may have accepted, until now, this interpretation of his character and felt ashamed. But now he is suddenly able to interpret his absorption in the building blocks as creativity and an early sign of his architectural vocation. Conversely, things that had previously been important – for example, his good head for figures – suddenly seem insignificant details. His meetings as a child with a rich uncle whom he had admired for holding a high position at a multi-national company likewise fade into the background, while the previously insignificant discovery of a book about the architect Gaudi in his father's bookshelf takes on the status of a landmark event. This is why Sartre can say that we choose not only our present and future but even our past:

> We choose the world – not in its contexture as in-itself, but in its meaning, by choosing ourselves. [21]

We find in the writing of history another example of how our future-related 'self-projections' can change the past. The historical events of antiquity are long since elapsed. No one can influence them any longer. And yet history is constantly rewritten. Even schoolbooks must be regularly re-edited. Because with every new social order and every new future-related idea there are also renewed and altered the criteria by which we judge and assess history itself.

Thus, when Germany was a divided nation, the historiography practiced in its eastern half was, due to the socialist project being pursued there, a quite different one from that practiced in the west. The 'self-projection' of the 'workers' and peasants' state' into a socialist future meant, for example, that the history of Alexander the Great was radically rewritten. While it was taught in West German schools and museums that the heroic Alexander had conquered, against great odds, the Persian army and created a mighty pan-Hellenic kingdom, the account conveyed by equivalent institutions in the East was that an imperialist driven by personal ambition had aggressed an entire continent: Alexander the First, son of Philip the Second, wrongly called 'The Great', had really done nothing but create, from the basest motives, a bloodbath with his army of mercenaries and irretrievably destroyed the unique palaces of Susa and Babylon; he had thereby annihilated centuries of effort by thousands of labouring people and proven himself to be a stupid barbarian; this empire he created by force of arms collapsed shortly after his death.

We see by this example how a society's new 'project' for itself can also revolutionize past history. Sartre says explicitly of the being of the past that:

[...] its meaning comes to it from the future [...]. Because the only force of the past comes to it from the future. [22]

Because then, this being the case, not even the past can in any way limit our freedom, Sartre feels able to reiterate his radical thesis that the human individual is restricted neither by his innate dispositions, nor by his upbringing, nor by his past life. He is and remains absolutely free:

Man is nothing other than his own project [...]. [23]

Sartre's Central Idea

"Bad Faith" ("Mauvaise Foi")

The past, then, has no power over us. Each time we 'project ourselves' anew into the future we see everything in a different light:

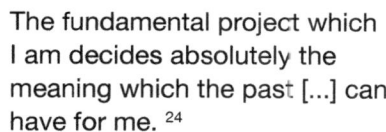

The fundamental project which I am decides absolutely the meaning which the past [...] can have for me. [24]

This is also why each of us is responsible for his own life. To try to evade this responsibility by citing such supposedly determining "facticities" as one's constitution, dispositions, background, or misfortunes one has suffered – this, argues Sartre, is 'bad faith'. (Sartre's original French here has gained some currency even among English-speaking existentialists and one sometimes hears this called '*mauvaise foi*'). Sartre be-

39

lieves that it is finally of no importance whether one was raised in a slum or a millionaire's villa, in a village or in a metropolis:

> (For) it is the future which decides whether the past is living or dead. [25]

It is often said of the poet Baudelaire that his life was ruined by early experiences and that, for this reason, 'he didn't have the life he deserved'. Sartre, of course, cannot accept such a view. Baudelaire, he argues, may indeed have been unhappy and lonely all his life; but he *chose* to be a man damned to loneliness. Baudelaire worshipped his mother. He loved her above all else. She was, for him, the justification of his whole existence. He felt eternally united with her. But when his mother remarried she sent him away to boarding school. This event was a watershed in the poet's life. He could not bear it that his beloved mother, instead of keeping him by her, remarried and threw him aside. Psychoanalysts, among others, have surmised that this lay at the root of Baudelaire's later difficulties in forming normal relationships with women. And indeed his sexual contacts were mostly with prostitutes; attempts to form relationships with other women all ended in tragic failure. Again and again, he found himself abandoned, deceived and lied to, just like in his childhood. In his confessional notebook *My Heart Laid Bare* we find him writing: "A sense of loneliness ever since my childhood. Despite my family – and above all amongst children of my own age – always the feeling of being fated to eternal solitude."

But Sartre criticises all this as mere excuses. The fact of separation, he argues, could not have been the cause of the poet's lifelong loneliness because he might also have chosen to take this early separation as the starting point for quite different kinds of 'self-projection': namely, as someone liberated into independence by it, or someone who responded to this experience of losing one dear human being by developing stronger rather than weaker bonds with the other human beings he encountered. But, instead of seeking out new friends, Baudelaire took this event as the starting point for an act of originary 'self-projection' as a lonely, abandoned individual. This (in Sartre's phrase) 'fundamental project' remains the clearly perceptible background and base of all the later 'self-projections' that make up the poet's life. Thus, the only relationships he later formed were with women whom he found repugnant, so as to prove to himself, through the failures this repugnance provoked, that for him all human ties were pointless. His loneliness, then, was his own *decision*:

He embraced it with fury, shut himself up in it and, since he was condemned to it, hoped that, at any rate, his condemnation was final. [26]

For Sartre, this meant that Baudelaire had fallen prey to 'mauvaise foi', 'bad faith'. Sartre takes a similar critical line regarding the theory of an 'inferiority complex' developed by the famous psychoanalyst

Adler. For Sartre, there is no 'inferiority complex', only an 'inferiority *choice*':

> Thus the inferiority which is felt and lived is the chosen instrument to make us comparable to a thing; that is, to make us exist as a pure outside in the midst of the world. [27]

But such a choice is cowardly, since one chooses, here, to be powerless so as to incur no danger of making false decisions and so as not to have to take responsibility. Sartre raises here the idea of a future refoundation of psychoanalysis in a more existentialist spirit. The task of such an existential psychoanalysis would be to recognize the particular 'fundamental project', the specific style of choice, that is governing the life of each patient and to try to inspire in each the courage to opt for a new and better orientation.

Nothingness

Sartre's work consists largely of a reiteration, in different ways, of his conviction that nothing at all can limit our freedom. But – and this is the 'flip side' of this absolute freedom – there is thereby also nothing at all helping us to master our own life, nothing telling us how we ought to live. Indeed – and this is perhaps the most threatening aspect – there is, in the end, nothing telling us *why we should live at all*. Because, as Sartre says:

> If *nothing* compels me to save my life, *nothing* prevents me from precipitating myself into the abyss. [28]

The decision to live, then, must be taken over and over again. Sartre was an atheist. He did not believe in God. If someone, in the midst of prayer or meditation, hears an 'inner voice' that tells them that, and how, they should live, or what is right or divinely ordained, this person is hearing, Sartre maintains, not the voice of any being outside themselves but only their own inner voice. This applies even when the person in question won't admit this and believes firmly in God. Because in the end, Sartre holds, it is of the very nature of the human being that he is condemned to take his decisions alone. No God, nor any 'higher power' of any kind, can do this for him since, in its inmost essence, human existence is based on *nothing*. Sartre was very deeply convinced of this. It is why he called his principal work of philosophy *Being and Nothingness*. And indeed, when we turn to consider this thing he calls 'nothingness' we attain to the very heart of Sartre's philosophy of existence. But what is 'nothingness'? Is it something that can really be experienced? Or is it just an abstract idea: the merely notional opposite of all that surrounds us in everyday life?

Sartre's answer here is amazing. Far from being a merely notional logical opposite of all that is present to us in daily life, nothingness can indeed be intensively experienced and concretely felt. It is in the concrete state of mind that Sartre calls 'anguish' that there becomes directly manifest to the human being that nothingness that he constantly bears about with him in the innermost core of his being:

> In anguish freedom is anguished before itself inasmuch as it is instigated and bound by nothing. [29]

Sartre draws a clear distinction here between the idea of anguish and that of fear. What inspires fear in us is always something concrete. We fear a dog that might bite, an examination, a storm, or an enemy. Anguish, on the other hand, often has no concrete object. We have a sense of being threatened, but here the threat is of a quite different nature. As Sartre writes:

> Anguish is distinguished from fear in that fear is fear of beings in the world whereas anguish is anguish before myself. [30]

Sartre clarifies this with the example of a soldier in the trenches who first feels only fear, before being overcome by the more fundamental feeling of anguish:

> The artillery preparation which precedes the attack can provoke fear in the soldier who undergoes the bombardment; but anguish is born in him when he tries to foresee the conduct with which he will face the bombardment, when he asks himself if he is going to be able to 'hold up'. [31]

Anguish, then, is essentially distinguished by being the anxiety that a human being feels about not being able to handle and master the tasks that face him in life. It is by no means only in such extreme situations as the one just described that we feel anguish. Even normal daily life can become a problem if human existence feels itself unable to address the tasks of this life with decision. Whether and in what way we do in fact address these tasks is entirely something we decide by exercising our freedom. Our absolute freedom, then, is at the same time the greatest of gifts and the basis of that fundamental dismay that is anguish:

> It is in anguish that Man gets the consciousness of his freedom [...]. It is in anguish that freedom is, in its being, in question for itself. [32]

Freedom and nothingness, then, are just two sides of the same coin; they are mutually determining. Human freedom is only absolute because it is limited by *nothing* – that is to say, because it is not until we decide in favour of life that we make ourselves what we are. Man must, therefore, project himself again and again, with decision, into *nothingness* and thereby again and again re-invent himself. Although we do this every day, this experience of nothingness remains, just the same, a source of anguish. Because, however, anguish confronts Man directly with himself, and with the *nothingness* at the core of his being, anguish cannot be derived from anything else. That is to say, anguish is not something that seizes us only at times. It is something primal and constant in us. Sartre writes simply and provocatively:

We *are* anguish. 33

But the question does indeed impose itself of why, if absolute freedom goes hand in hand with a feeling of anguish in the face of nothingness, we do not live every day in a constant state of anguish. Sartre poses this question himself:

If anguish manifests (freedom), then anguish ought to be a permanent state of my affectivity. But, on the contrary, it is completely exceptional. How can we explain the rarity of the phenomenon of anguish? 34

Sartre's answer is simple. In everyday life we make our decisions by choosing, in routine manner, from among different possibilities that one which seems most advantageous. Anguish never arises because we never become aware of that dimension of nothingness which alone makes possible this latitude of individual decision. And even when a decision proves difficult and a feeling of anguish does seem about to arise, we usually quickly suppress it by deciding as we see others decide, following the advice of others, or just deciding, for convenience's sake, to make the 'normal' decision for each situation. But this does not change the fact that every decision, in the end, is a *creatio ex nihilo*, a decision grounded in nothingness:

Freedom is precisely the nothingness which is *made-to-be* at the heart of Man and which forces human reality to *make itself* instead of to *be*. [35]

'Looking' and 'Being-Looked-At'

With the idea of absolute freedom as the experience of nothingness we have expressed the central idea of Sartre's philosophy of existence. But, astonishingly, Sartre also raises, in *Being and Nothingness*, a second and in many ways even more exciting question: namely, the question as to the role of other human beings. What role does our 'fellow man' play in this drama of individual human existence? Does 'the other individual' provide us with some purchase and support here? How exactly do we perceive this 'other'? Might 'the other' even constitute that limitation on my freedom that nothing else can? With his analysis of 'being-for-others' Sartre was, in fact, one of the very first thinkers to engage intensively with the structure of the relations existing *between* human being and human being. For millennia, philosophers tended to concentrate on exploring how the *individual human being* thinks, feels and acts. Sartre, by contrast, is one of the first to attentively examine the question of how men and women relate to *other men and women* and to pose the fascinating question: what are the key structures of *inter-human relationships*?

We find Sartre making a first attempt to clarify the basis of all human inter-relations, and thereby the structure of 'being-for-others', with his brilliant phenomenological analyses of 'the look'. When he speaks of 'the look' Sartre means not so much the physical ability to see and be seen as the *feeling* of the presence of 'the Other'. If, for example, while seeing nothing at all, we hear a rustling in the bushes behind us, we might feel that we are being looked at, since something indicates the close presence of someone who may be drawing us, in some way unknown to us, into his own project – be this the project of a thief who may rob us, a friend who will greet us, or a person so involved in his own action that he will ignore us as we pass by.

It is through looking and being looked at, Sartre believes, that we most clearly experience the truth that 'the Other' is in no way just another ordinary object among all the various objects we encounter in our daily life. For example, when I am sitting relaxing on a park bench, I have no problem grouping the path, the lawn, the flowers, the benches and the other objects I perceive, one by one, in terms of their respective distances from me and their positions vis-à-vis one another.

But as soon as another person comes walking by, I experience something strange. Somehow it proves impossible to maintain my earlier way of looking at things and to slot this newly-appearing human being into my ordering and classification of the things around me as if he were a puppet or some other inanimate object:

If I were to think of him as being only a puppet, I should apply to him the categories I ordinarily use to group spatio-temporal 'things'. That is, I should apprehend him as being 'beside' the benches, two yards and twenty inches from the lawn, as exercising a certain pressure on the ground etc. His relation with other objects would be of the purely additive type; this means that I could have him disappear without the relations of the other objects around him being perceptibly changed. [36]

But this seems suddenly to be no longer possible and I am forced to recognize that the things that I have been able, up till now, to group and order so effortlessly have acquired, through the appearance of this other human being, new relations and significances that I am unable to control. The lawn on which he is walking, the bench he is walking toward, now seem, oddly, to derive their meaning, and their respective distances, from this strange 'Other'. A new space has taken form around this 'Other' and this space has been made, without my permission, from my space:

There is a regrouping in which I take part but which escapes me. 37

This strolling 'Other' thereby proves himself to be in no way just an object which can be fitted into my perceived environment like any other object; rather, it is this (in Sartre's phrase) "privileged object that is the Other" who sets about re-ordering what is now *his* world. There has thus suddenly become visible, with this appearance of the 'Other', an object which has stolen the world away from me:

Sartre's Central Idea

> Everything is still in place; everything still exists for me; but everything is traversed by an invisible flight and fixed in the direction of a new object. The appearance of the 'Other' in the world corresponds, therefore [...] to a decentralization of the world which undermines the centralization which I am simultaneously effecting. [38]

The 'Other' is thus, Sartre concludes:

> [...] the permanent flight of things toward a goal which I apprehend as an object at a certain distance from me but which escapes me inasmuch as it unfolds about itself its own distances. [39]

Furthermore, the 'Other' acquires a still greater significance for me if I bear in mind that this 'Other' not only orders and organizes the world as he sees it according to his own projects and interests but also draws *me* into his world as well. "The privileged *object* that is the Other" suddenly becomes "the *subject* that is the Other". He is experienced as such by me through what Sartre calls my "permanent possibility of *being-looked-at-by-him*". That is to say, through this 'being-looked-at-by-him' I grasp the 'Other' as a subject but I am, at the same time, thrown back upon myself and become 'fixed'. I am 'fixed' inasmuch as I cannot now escape whatever meaning the 'Other' ascribes to me. Sartre elucidates this notion by reference to the phenomenon of shame.

Sartre's Central Idea

Shame Under the "Look of the Other"

> Let us imagine that, moved by jealousy, curiosity or vice, I have just glued my ear to the door and looked through a keyhole [...]. All of a sudden I hear footsteps in the hall. Someone is looking at me! What does this mean? It means that I am suddenly affected in my being and that essential modifications appear in my structure – modifications which I can apprehend and fix conceptually by means of the reflective cogito. [40]

The 'Other' catches me by surprise and freezes my own understanding of myself, fixing it as the self-understanding of an eavesdropper or voyeur. As someone experiencing such a 'being-looked-at-by-the-Other' I am seized by shame. And through this shame that I feel under the 'Other''s look, I experience myself as 'fixed' by him in a single identity. The 'Other' sees me, in this moment, solely and exclusively as a curious or jealous voyeur. He robs me, as it were, of all the other possibilities which might, above and beyond this, be at the disposal of my 'I'. Under the 'Other''s look, my whole being is reduced to this single attitude that I have just adopted: that of the voyeur. This look, in other words, instantaneously petrifies my freedom. Sartre refers here to the myth of Medusa, who turned anyone who looked into her eyes to stone. This myth, Sartre suggests, gives expression to the phenomenon that we necessarily always feel ourselves to be objectified by the 'look of the Other'. In the very moment in which it strikes me, this look fixes or binds me to a specific appearing image of myself and refuses to me all other possibilities. It thereby reduces me to the condition of an 'in-itself': something which merely 'is what it is'.

But at the same time, Sartre goes on, I also learn through this experience of 'being-seen-by-the-Other' that it is actually impossible for me to be entirely comprised and subsumed in this condition of mere 'being-in-itself' which the look of the 'Other' ascribes to me. I experience the greatest possible discomfort in this situation and this discomfort is an expression of the fact that it is actually impossible for me to become just a pure object. That is to say, I cannot completely accept this idea of myself as a mere voyeur.

Sartre's Central Idea

Everything in me resists this ascription. I wish to be, and am, more than this. Because a human being is indeed never simply a thing that 'is what it is'; a human being is, as Sartre says, 'being-*for*-itself'; that is to say, he is a presence *to* himself; he stands in a relation to himself; and it is in this that his freedom inheres. A human being is never *only* that which he is doing at any moment, or that which others observe him to be doing when their look happens to strike him. A human being is constantly in upheaval.

This being that is 'for-itself', then, can never be fully comprised and subsumed in this state of 'being-a-voyeur', even if the 'for-itself' is forced, in the moment of being caught by the look of the 'Other', to see himself thus and only thus. Hence the feeling of shame. Philosophically formulated, the phenomenon of shame means: despite that transcendence that is proper to my own being, I am compelled by another transcendence to identify myself with that 'in-itself' which a freedom which is not my freedom happens, in the moment of its looking at me, to see me as. If I did not feel recognized in this look, I would not feel shame either. The 'Other', then, calls forth an effect in me. Shame, in the end, is only an expression of the event of my recognizing my own self in the look of the 'Other'. Whereas at first, while I am alone and preoccupied by my own spying at the door, it never occurs to me that I am objectively a voyeur, in the moment of 'being-looked-at' I recognize myself all the more jarringly as just that. From this phenomenological observation Sartre draws a radical conclusion:

> Pure shame is not a feeling of being this or that guilty object but in general of being an object; that is, of recognizing *myself* in this degraded, fixed and dependent being which I am for the Other. [41]

Consequently, Sartre argues, the look is, in its essence, a pure reference back to myself, because it is only in the look of the 'Other' that I form an image of myself. I need and require, indeed, this 'look of the Other' in order to achieve selfhood at all, since I can only become an object of my own consciousness in and through becoming aware of the awareness that *others* have of me. The image I have of myself is one that is reflected back to me from the 'Other'. This is why others' judgments of us – whether they find us attractive or repulsive, pleasant or unpleasant, clever or stupid – are important to us. The way I exist for myself is, to a great extent, the way I exist for others, so that my identity depends intimately upon these latter:

By virtue of consciousness the Other is, for me, simultaneously the one who has stolen my being from me and the one who causes 'there to be' a being which is my being. [42]

'Being-looked-at' means, first and foremost, to grasp oneself as an object of unknowable judgments. To 'be looked at' is to be an object for the 'Other'. But because the 'Other' is free I can never know in advance, with any certainty, how he will judge me. This is the case even though I am radically dependent on such judgment by the 'Other' for my own self-knowledge:

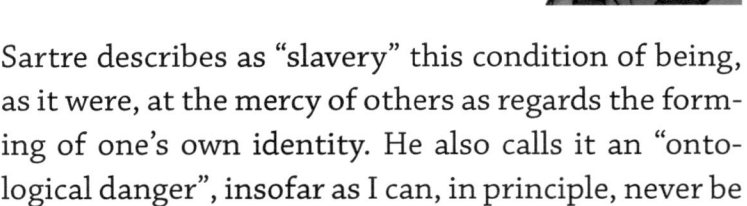

> Thus, 'being-seen' constitutes me as a defenceless being for a freedom which is not my freedom. It is in this sense that we can consider ourselves 'slaves' insofar as we appear to the 'Other'. [...] I am a slave to the extent that I am dependent, in the depth of my being, on a freedom which is not mine but which is nonetheless the very condition of my being. [43]

Sartre describes as "slavery" this condition of being, as it were, at the mercy of others as regards the forming of one's own identity. He also calls it an "ontological danger", insofar as I can, in principle, never be sure of being recognized by these others:

> I am in danger [...]. And this danger is not an accident but the permanent structure of my being-for-others. [44]

Now, in view of this constant uncertainty one might be tempted to simply disregard the judgment of others, declaring: 'it doesn't matter to me what others think of me'. But Sartre considers such a stance to be impossible because it is only through engagement with others, and through the reflection in myself of the look that they direct at me, that I acquire a sense of my own selfhood. I can, however, Sartre concedes, endeavour to appear to the 'Other' in such a way that the image of me that he forms as part of his own 'project' is one that corresponds to my own wished-for image of myself.

"Being-For-Others" as Struggle for Recognition

Sartre sees there to follow from these analyses of 'the look' a certain unavoidable paradox of human existence. On the one hand, it is only in and through recognition by others that the individual human being comes to know himself *as* a 'self'; on the other hand, he fears this recognition (or its withholding) as an objectification and petrification of his possibilities:

> Shame is the feeling of an *original fall*, not because of the fact that I may have committed this or that particular fault but simply that I have 'fallen' into the world in the midst of things and that I need the mediation of the Other in order to be what I am. [45]

The author too (to take a favourite example of Sartre's) always requires, in order to be what he is, the recognition of his readers. Thus, his work only becomes a work of art, and he himself a 'writer' as opposed to someone who merely 'writes things down', in and through the 'look' of others. Literature, he says, requires the united effort of author and reader. Art exists only for and through the 'Other'. But I can never be certain of being recognized by the 'Other' inasmuch as I am dependent here on a freedom that is not my own.

It is also against this background of the "ontological danger" that inheres in 'being-looked-at' that we can understand the phenomenon of 'stage fright'. In most people's cases these situations of seeking recognition in the 'look of the Other' arise and pass almost unnoticeably as part of everyday life. But the case of the actor is interesting because he has made it his profession to expose himself to these 'looks'. The Shakespearian sentiment that 'all the world's a stage' is doubly true for those of Shakespeare's own trade. The judgment an audience passes on what it sees on stage is not just a judgment passed on the credibility of a fictional world. It is also a judgment passed on the skill of those whose efforts *make* this world credible and thereby on the *real* world of the working actor.

In the light of Sartre's analysis of 'the look' it is easy to understand why actors experience 'stage fright' as a state of diffuse excitation in which anguish and pleasure are indissolubly mixed. On the one hand, the actor can hardly wait to appear before his audience, looking forward to thunderous waves of applause; on the other, the thought of the 'look' of this very same audience casts him into anguish. Because this audience might shame him to the bone and annihilate him with boos and whistles. Even when an actor has learnt his lines perfectly and possesses all the skills required to play his role, the thought alone of the audience, with its high expectations and unpredictable moods, can suffice to cause him 'stage fright'. This unpredictability of the recognition we derive from the 'look of the Other' is, says Sartre, a reality which we sometimes try to escape by creating conditions in which our recognition by the 'Other' seems securely guaranteed:

> We have observed that the Other's freedom is the foundation of my being. But precisely because I exist by means of the Other's freedom, I have no security; I am in danger in this freedom. It moulds my being and

Sartre's Central Idea

> *makes me be*; it confers values upon me and removes them from me. [...] My project of recovering my being can be realized only if I get hold of this freedom and reduce it to being a freedom subject to my freedom. [46]

The tyrant, for example, secures the recognition of others by depriving them of their freedom and compelling them to recognize him as a significant person. Admittedly, such a forced recognition is of little value in the end, precisely because it is forced. The same advisers and vassals as laud him in his presence speak ill of him in his absence, when they have nothing more to fear. What is more, the dictator knows this. His true objectification remains hidden from him, so that he remains in a constant state of insecurity after all.

But there exists, argues Sartre, a much shrewder path than the path of power and tyranny by which one might attempt to secure for oneself the recognition of the 'Other': namely, love. Because love, phenomenologically considered, is the bizarre enterprise of acquiring, from another human being, a recognition which is at the same time voluntary and unconditional.

Love as the Surmounting of Struggle?

The idea of love is thus, initially, a very simple one for Sartre. The attempt is made to permanently subjugate to oneself a freedom which, even in its subjugation, will continue, freely and repeatedly, to recognize and confirm one's own being. If such an enterprise succeeds, the 'look of the Other' loses its aspect of threat, which is replaced by a wonderful feeling. Where the 'look of the Other' becomes a 'look of love' alone, I experience a recognition that is uplifting because it is unconditional. Each person in a love relationship seeks and finds security, even in their freedom, in the other. They allow themselves to be made part of the other's free 'project', secure in the knowledge that this 'project' will be one engaged in for their sake. They are thereby freed from the threatening nothingness of existence as the 'for-itself', since they are now no longer under the necessity or creating their own being ever anew out of their own essential nothingness:

> Whereas before being loved we were uneasy about that unjustified, unjustifiable protruberance which was our existence, whereas we felt ourselves 'de trop',

> we now feel that our existence is taken up and willed even in its tiniest details by an absolute freedom [...]. This is the basis for the joy of love, when there is joy: we feel that our existence is justified. [47]

Love is essentially the project of making myself loved or also of wanting that the 'Other' should want to be loved by me. The lover undertakes everything in their power to bring it about that the 'Other' desires them as a privileged object in their (the 'Other''s) world and that this 'Other' recognizes them, in the last analysis, as a freedom that cannot be transcended:

> Thus, to want to be loved is to infect the Other with one's own facticity; it is the wish to compel him to recreate you perpetually. [48]

But how can I oblige a freedom that is not my own to perpetually validate and recreate me in this way? I do so, says Sartre, by making myself, for the 'Other', the utmost fullness of being, the most meaningful of all objects – that is, by attempting to become, for this 'Other', "the whole world". When the 'Other' does indeed declare, in the face of my plenitude of being: "You are my world", I appear to have achieved my aim. This is why Sartre concludes:

> Seduction aims at producing in the 'Other' the consciousness of his state of nothingness as he confronts the seductive object. [49]

That is to say, I make it my project to become a "seductive object", a being of "endless depth", in the hope of charming the 'Other' and affecting this 'Other''s freedom to such an extent that this free being becomes so fascinated by my person as to willingly let themselves be put in chains. As opposed to the dictator, who uses violence to compel the 'Other' to recognize and validate him, the lover wishes to charm the 'Other' and to draw a voluntary recognition from this 'Other' through the uncompelling bonds of love:

> Thus, the lover does not desire to possess the beloved as one possesses a thing; he demands a special type of appropriation. He wants to possess a freedom as freedom. [50]

If this succeeds, as I must hope it will when I become a lover, I secure for myself a recognition by the 'Other' that is voluntary and yet at the same time permanent and dependable. It is a recognition which allows me, after I have been obliged to 'go out of myself' as object for the 'look of the Other', to 'return into myself' once again, and to do so, moreover, in exactly the form and image in which I had originally wished to. Since this freedom of the 'Other' has now become one that is dependent on me, this freedom will draw me into its own free 'project' in just the way I wish to be drawn into it. I will receive compliments and encouragement, and even if the 'Other' criticizes me, it will be affectionate, benevolent criticism. The project, then, of securing the recognition of the 'Other' by the path of inspiring love appears at first sight to be a very promising one. But Sartre shows that even this tempting enterprise is doomed, in the end, to fail:

> I demand that the Other love me and I do everything possible to realize my project; but if the other loves me back, he radically disappoints me through this very love. I demanded of him that he should found my being as a privileged object by maintaining himself as pure subjectivity confronting me. But as soon as he loves me he experiences me as subject and is swallowed up in his objectivity confronting my subjectivity. [51]

We find clearly stated here the paradox that tends to lead to the failure of love. I can indeed secure myself a loving recognition in and through the 'look' of a beloved person by making myself a "privileged object" in his or her world, that is, an object to which this person becomes completely attached. But precisely where I succeed in doing this, the recognition that I receive will be one that arises out of amorous dependency and no longer out of true freedom. The recognition received thereby loses all value. In other words: so long as the 'Other' does not love me, he is free; but as soon as he begins to love me, his freedom vanishes.

The project of the lover is bound to fail, then, whichever way he tackles it. On the one hand he must be careful, in his attempt to secure permanent voluntary recognition by the 'Other', not to make this latter emotionally dependent on (let alone subservient to) him, since this would be to rob the 'Other' of his freedom.

But on the other hand, he cannot simply leave the 'Other''s freedom untouched, because then whether to grant recognition or not would be a matter of the 'Other''s spontaneous decision and the lover would have the problem of never being able to be sure of his partner's attitude:

The attempt, then, to escape, by recourse to love, the ontological danger that is the 'Other''s refusal of recognition is an attempt that is doomed to failure. But the promise that love seems to hold out of placing one's existence in safety through the loving recognition of the 'Other' is such a fine one that it is understandable why people make this attempt again and again. Still, in the end, argues Sartre, since we both fear objectification by the 'Other' but at the same time need it if we are truly to experience our own selfhood, there is for Man no escape from struggle and conflict:

Sartre's Central Idea

Conflict is the original meaning of 'being-for-others'. 53

Man remains perpetually dependent on that recognition of his own selfhood which he finds only in the look with which he responds to the 'look of the Other'. That is to say, he remains perpetually dependent on the judgment of others. Not even love can offer us a way out of this dynamic.

Absolute Freedom and Absolute Responsibility

How, then, is this notion to be reconciled with Sartre's philosophy of absolute freedom? If I cannot escape my dependence on 'the look of the Other', am I really free at all? But Sartre sees no contradiction here. For even if the 'Other''s judgment is able to 'turn me to stone', it cannot really limit my freedom. Because I am able at any time to alter, through my decisions and my actions, the image that others have formed of me. This is why Sartre holds to his basic proposition that:

Man is nothing other than what he makes of himself. This is the first principle of existentialism. [54]

Man is free – and not only in the sense that freedom belongs to him as a possibility but in the sense that each man is himself this freedom. Freedom is an existential fact. Our condition of being "condemned to be free" is something we can never shake off. Nor can the 'Other' relieve the individual of the task of free decision. Each person, then, is and remains responsible for his being.

It is only in his late work entitled *Critique of Dialectical Reason* that Sartre slightly revises this position and accords somewhat more weight to the material circumstances of a person's life. As a left intellectual, he wanted to reconcile existentialism with Marxism and bring out some points in common between them. Thus Sartre concedes in this late work to the Marxists that work, the material relations of production and the historical epoch into which individuals are born do in fact have great influence on the existence of each individual. Karl Marx's famous proposition: "social being determines consciousness" is partially accepted by Sartre here after all. He no longer emphasizes, therefore, in this second main statement of his ideas, the absolute freedom of the individual as strongly as he had done in *Being and Nothingness*, conceding greater significance to the marks left on this individual by society. The idea of freedom as limitless "self-projection" and *creatio ex nihilo* is, in Sartre's last years, propounded only in conditional form:

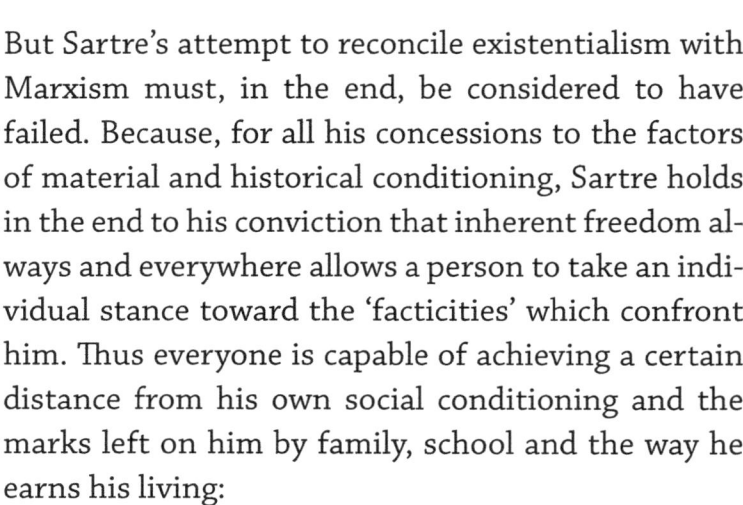

Freedom (is) the small movement that makes of a totally conditioned social being someone who does not render back completely what his conditioning has given him. [55]

But Sartre's attempt to reconcile existentialism with Marxism must, in the end, be considered to have failed. Because, for all his concessions to the factors of material and historical conditioning, Sartre holds in the end to his conviction that inherent freedom always and everywhere allows a person to take an individual stance toward the 'facticities' which confront him. Thus everyone is capable of achieving a certain distance from his own social conditioning and the marks left on him by family, school and the way he earns his living:

Sartre's Central Idea

I believe that a man can always make something out of what is made of him. [56]

Sartre is and remains, then, the philosopher of freedom who tirelessly admonishes us and reminds us that we are ourselves responsible for what we think and do.

Of What Use Is Sartre's Discovery for Us Today?

Leave "Bad Faith" Behind – Go Your Own Way

Freedom is absolute, regardless of whether one is a man or a woman, rich or poor, born in a village or in the big city. Such is the credo of existentialism. Even as a prisoner in chains, Sartre argues, I am no less free than anyone else, since it is, in the end, my decision what attitude I take to the facts of my situation:

> Freedom is total and infinite [...]. The only limits which freedom bumps up against at each moment are those which it imposes on itself. [57]

Sartre uses the example of "a boulder in the road" to clarify this. A boulder will block the road only for the person who resigns himself to being blocked, not for the person who looks on the obstacle as a challenge to climb over it or find a way around it. From this perspective we even choose to be born or to die, since we freely decide what value we are going to ascribe to birth and death and how far we will make these events significant individual concerns for ourselves. Thus Sartre admonishes us over and over again to form and fashion our lives with decisiveness:

You are nothing but your life. [58]

In the end, what counts is what you do. This sounds at first like a banal truism. But on closer consideration Sartre's simple appeal to us to act instead of hiding behind excuses and self-deceptions is perhaps the most important part of existentialism's legacy. Because we are all familiar with the problem of "bad faith": that is, the avoidance of honesty with oneself. One often feels unsatisfied with certain aspects of one's life – be it one's relations with one's partner, one's work, one's family, one's home, or with the political and social circumstances around one – yet still leaves these things unchanged. One prefers to invent a thousand reasons why 'one's hands are tied' instead of actually doing something. Sartre advises us to carefully examine whether, when we choose our ends, we are taking genuine decisions and not just yielding to "bad faith", that is to say, to the failure to be true to ourselves, or self-deception:

[...] the responsibility for these ends falls on us. Whatever our being may be, it is a choice; and it depends on us to choose ourselves as 'great' and 'noble' or as 'base' and 'humiliated'. [59]

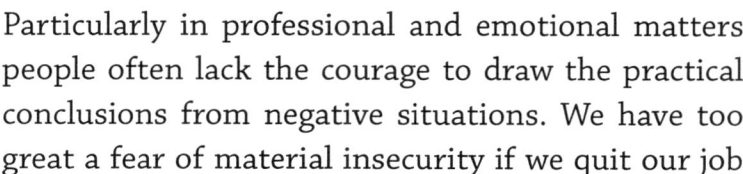

Particularly in professional and emotional matters people often lack the courage to draw the practical conclusions from negative situations. We have too great a fear of material insecurity if we quit our job and of crushing loneliness if we leave a long-term partner. Indeed, long-term relationships tend to be characterized by a clear 'division of labour', precisely defined routines, and a well-practiced 'role-playing' which make a shared life bearable. This is why many relationships continue to function even when emotional closeness is no longer there and even when tensions between the partners have begun to emerge. It is this that Sartre calls "bad faith", or self-deception.

Sartre himself tried to rule out, from the very start, the risk of sustaining a relationship lacking in authenticity and based on a multitude of big and small lies. He did this by making a pact of freedon and openness with his lifelong companion Simone de Beauvoir. In an exchange of letters each assured the other of their constant and lifelong love without consenting thereby to robbing themselves of their respective freedoms. They agreed that they could each have other partners and affairs but that this would never lead them to lie to or neglect each other. Simone de Beauvoir later wrote: "Sartre was not inclined to be monogamous by nature; he took pleasure in the company of women [...]. He had no intention, at twenty-three, of renouncing their tempting variety. He explained the matter to me in his favourite terminology: 'What we have,' he said, 'is an *essential* love; but it is a good idea for us also to experience *contingent* love affairs.' We were two of a kind and our relationship would endure as long as we did." [60]

And the two did indeed remain a couple their whole lives, despite many openly-conducted affairs with 'contingent loves', and were able always to rely on each other. The formula for this lasting partnership was their common fidelity to freedom. They avoided ever marrying and thus, as it were, 'chose each other' every day anew.

Although this relationship was much admired by the couple's contemporaries, even it encountered strains and problems whenever one of the 'contingent loves' became too lasting or strong a presence. But whether or not Sartre actually succeeded in always maintaining this balance of absolute honesty and absolute trust in his relationship with de Beauvoir, his constant aspiration remained nonetheless to be veracious with himself and others, to stand by his own failures and weaknesses, and to reject all facile and merely apparent solutions.

When Sartre exhorts us to be open and honest he does not, of course, mean that we should be fanatical tellers of the exact truth in our everyday interaction and never tell a 'white lie'. If scientific studies are to be believed, such behaviour would be simply unfeasible, since most people have no choice but to tell many such 'white lies' daily if they are not to give offence to those around them. Sartre's message to us regarding honesty, then, is not: "Always tell the literal truth" but rather: "Be honest with yourself and live your life."

Don't Just Dream – Put Your Thoughts and Ideas into Practice

This is exactly why it is important to put one's thoughts and ideas into practice:

Man is nothing other than what he makes of himself. [61]

It is useless, argues Sartre, to merely dream of living a different life and useless to be unsatisfied with the social system one lives in if one does not take steps to change it. One must, when the time is ripe, stand up and be counted and attempt to make one's vision a reality. Because otherwise, when one's life is drawing to a close, one will have to admit to oneself that one has not followed what was perhaps one's true vocation. One often tells oneself that life is too short to do everything one's inner voice prompts one to do. But Sartre does not accept this way of thinking either:

> One always dies too soon – or too late. And yet your life is there, completed. The line is drawn, you have to add up the figures. You are your life and only your life. [62]

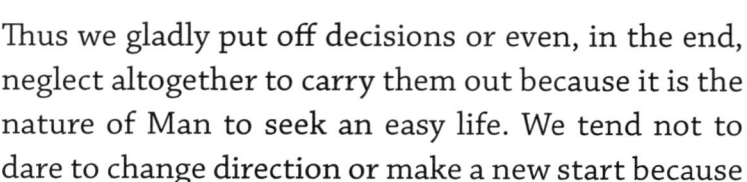

Thus we gladly put off decisions or even, in the end, neglect altogether to carry them out because it is the nature of Man to seek an easy life. We tend not to dare to change direction or make a new start because we are scared of losing those routine comforts that we have become so fond of. Nevertheless, Sartre urges us to follow those paths that best express our true selves:

> The first effect of existentialism is to make every man conscious of what he is and to make him solely responsible for his own existence. [63]

And even if, sometimes, these paths turn out to be 'dead ends', or our expectations fail to be realized, we will still have done the right thing in daring to act. Better to fail than never to try at all.

This existential decisiveness even in the face of the possibility of failure is beautifully expressed in the film *Zorba the Greek*. The adventurous Zorba convinces his English friend to invest his last pennies in a kind of chute, constructed with struts of wood, intended to carry felled logs down from a mountaintop into the valley. As soon as the first logs slide down the chute the struts begin to sway and quiver. Zorba and his friend watch anxiously. Finally, the whole row of struts collapses, one after the other in a chain reaction. The Englishman is ruined. But Zorba merely asks his depressed friend: "Did you ever see anything fall so beautifully?" and begins to dance.

Expressed in Sartre's categories, Zorba simply commits himself here, even in the moment of defeat, once again to his own 'project' and to the failure that belongs to it. Sartre, of course, does not intend to make failure something heroic in itself. On the contrary, as a philosopher of freedom he is convinced that we all have a chance of achieving the goal that we set ourselves.

Sartre himself was barely five foot tall and suffered, from childhood on, from a noticeable optical defect. These traits made him an object of mockery throughout his earliest years. But he resolved nonetheless already at age fourteen to become an author and tenaciously pursued this once-conceived life-project until he did indeed achieve worldwide fame. He came also regularly to be seen, besides with his main female companion Simone de Beauvoir, also in the company of many other attractive women. This striking success in bringing his personal life-project to realization may partly explain why he assigned such great significance and value to human freedom.

Interestingly, modern research into the psychology of human happiness lends support to Sartre's views at least on this point. People who have changed something in their lives and have taken risks thereby tend to feel, subjectively, happier than people who have not. Clearly, besides money, general prosperity, health, prestige, and social relations, 'readiness to take risks' is another significant factor in people's happiness. And even if the risk does not 'pay off', and failure or disaster ensue, we can always, Sartre argues, take our lives in a better direction once again through new decisions and actions. Once again, this was an experience which Sartre himself underwent on more than one occasion.

If Necessary, Be Ready to Rethink

Because Sartre certainly took his share of intellectual and ethical 'wrong turnings'. As an intellectual he belonged to the left, fighting against social inequality and sympathizing with the Communist Party. He made well-publicized visits to the Soviet Union and even, at one point, lent his support to Stalin's policies of 'purifying' party and state of his political enemies. This latter was a decision which he came later deeply to regret.

During the Cold War, Sartre's positive stance toward the Soviet Union even led to a quarrel with his friend Albert Camus. Camus – like Sartre, an author of both philosophy and literature and, like Sartre, called an existentialist – mounted, in the summer of 1952, a critique of Stalin's brutal policies, above all his arrest and murder of thousands of his political opponents. The work-camps in which these people were imprisoned were, said Camus, indefensible. The system in the USSR was mere dictatorship.

Sartre vehemently contradicted these views of his former political ally, accusing Camus of anti-communism and bourgeois sentimentality. Stalin and the other Soviet leaders, he argued, had no choice but to take such measures in order to defend themselves against the reactionary capitalist forces. Sartre himself, indeed, condemned Stalin's prison-camps but insisted that a positive development of the Soviet system could be expected in the longer term. Where Camus condemned oppression in the Eastern bloc countries as uncompromisingly as he did in the West, Sartre demanded that "a distinction be drawn between the different 'masters'". It was socialism, Sartre argued, that would eventually bring an end to oppression everywhere in the world; he was unwilling, therefore, to say anything to discredit the state that he saw as the driving force behind this eventual global triumph of socialism: the Soviet Union. This difference of stance between Camus and Sartre led to a violent polemic conducted between the two men in the pages of Sartre's magazine *Les Temps Modernes*.

Sartre accused Camus of betraying, with his anti-communist stance, the very idea of a more just society. He also charged that Camus' particular form of existentialism – his "philosophy of the absurd" – meant that he saw reality completely non-historically, so that he was unable even to order political events properly, let alone comprehend them. Camus, on his side, accused Sartre of using the principle that 'the end justifies the means' to lend legitimacy to mass murder. A revolutionary movement built on the bodies of masses of people, argued Camus, could never really be legitimate, because the 'real humanism' aimed at by socialists cannot be achieved by trampling on human rights. Sartre's Marxism, Camus charged, was a terroristic doctrine of earthly salvation which excused all present horrors with the promise of a perfect future. He furthermore allowed himself the personal criticism that Sartre was unwilling even to look for truth in any camp but the left. This polemic was so bitter that the two former friends avoided all further contact from that time on.

But a few years later in November 1956, when Soviet tanks violently quelled the uprising of the Hungarian people, Sartre recognized that he had been wrong. He publicly recanted his pro-Soviet stance, condemned the Stalinist regime, and firmly distanced himself from the Communist Party. This complete reversal of his position certainly wasn't easy for him. But Sartre was willing to adapt his ideas to new developments and openly admitted his mistake. Such errors of judgment, he confessed at the age of 70, are simply a part of life:

> The important thing for me is that what had to be done was done. For better or worse, it doesn't matter. In any case, I've given it a try. [64]

When we ask ourselves 'of what use is Sartre's philosophy to us today?' we should perhaps not overlook this ability shown by the existentialist to rethink his own ideas.

Become Political – The Courage to Intervene

Sartre's philosophy of freedom contained above all an appeal that we commit ourselves to the cause of making the world more just than it presently is:

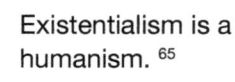

Existentialism is a humanism. [65]

In the famous lecture of this name Sartre develops the argument that a basic concern for every existentialist must also be the general welfare of society. Sartre gave and published this lecture to defend himself against the charge brought by Marxists that existentialism was an immoral pseudo-philosophy which aimed only at encouraging the private self-development of the individual. In Sartre's vision of a "free, future-oriented self-projection" of each individual – so ran the Marxist critique – there was no place at all for class consciousness, collective actions of solidarity, or indeed even for sympathy with the fate of others. Sartre vigorously repudiated this critique:

> And when we say that Man is responsible for himself, we do not mean that he is responsible only for his own individuality but that he is responsible for all men [...]. Choosing to be this or that is to affirm at the same time the value of what we choose. [66]

By choosing and acting the way we do day by day, we create an image of ourselves. Someone, for example, who drives a car with a 20-litre engine, uses fossil fuels, wears fur coats made from the pelts of endangered species, and destabilizes national economies through currency speculation makes something known about himself, through his particular 'life-project', for which he must bear responsibility. Like a painter, we add, with every decision, one more small stroke to our 'life-image'. This image or style of life, be it negative or positive, that we live out, as it were, before our children, friends and acquaintances, is never without consequences:

> If [...] we fashion our image, that image is valid for all and for our whole era. Our responsibility is thus much greater than we might have supposed, because it concerns all Mankind. [67]

This is the reason why every apparently merely private commitment has, in fact, significance for society – be it "only" a decision on how to raise one's children or even on whether or not to separate the refuse in one's dustbin. When Sartre writes about "commitment", then, he is not referring just to political agitation in parties, NGOs, unions, and other organizations and associations. He means individual actions as well, since these latter, taken together, do decidedly have an effect on society:

Consequently, every project, however individual, has a universal value. [68]

It was Sartre's view that each individual human being has, by reason of his freedom, to enjoy the free capacity to contribute in his own personal way to the success and welfare of society. Because every future-oriented self-projection, however apparently individual, changes the world as a whole and gives meaning to this world. Admittedly, the individual cannot expect help from anyone in this search for meaning: neither from a God, nor from an ideology, nor even from a science. For – to reiterate Sartre's central idea – our existence is, in the last analysis, grounded in nothingness. And this means that nothing and no one is there to relieve us of the task of giving meaning to our lives. This is the key proposition that Sartre insists on once again, with special emphasis, toward the conclusion of his famous lecture *Existentialism Is a Humanism*:

> Life has no meaning *a priori*. Life itself is nothing until it is lived. It is we who give it meaning. [69]

Bibliographical References:

1. Jean-Paul Sartre, Existentialism is a Humanism, Yale University Press 2007, p. 29
2. Ibid. p.22.
3. Ibid. p. 23
4. Jean-Paul Sartre, Being and Nothingness, Routledge Classics 2002, p. 552
5. Ibid. p. 388
6. Ibid. p. 386
7. Ibid. p. 49
8. Jean-Paul Sartre, Existentialism is a Humanism, Yale University Press 2007, p. 37
9. Jean-Paul Sartre, Being and Nothingness, Routledge Classics 2002, p. 584
10. Jean-Paul Sartre, Existentialism is a Humanism, Yale University Press 2007, p. 29
11. Jean-Paul Sartre, Being and Nothingness, Routledge Classics 2002, p. 516
12. Ibid. p. 494
13. Ibid.
14. Jean-Paul Sartre, Existentialism is a Humanism, Yale University Press 2007, p. 45
15. Jean-Paul Sartre, Being and Nothingness, Routledge Classics 2002, p. 49
16. Jean-Paul Sartre, Existentialism is a Humanism, Yale University Press 2007, p. 46
17. Ibid. p. 49
18. Ibid. p. 23
19. Jean-Paul Sartre, Being and Nothingness, Routledge Classics 2002, p. 21
20. Ibid. pps. 519-20
21. Ibid. p. 485
22. Ibid. p. 520-21
23. Jean-Paul Sartre, Existentialism is a Humanism, Yale University Press 2007, p. 37

24 Jean-Paul Sartre, Being and Nothingness, Routledge Classics 2002, p. 519
25 Ibid. p. 520
26 Jean-Paul Sartre, Baudelaire, New Directions Books, 1950, p. 18
27 Jean-Paul Sartre, Being and Nothingness, Routledge Classics 2002, p. 494
28 Ibid. p. 56
29 Ibid. p. 59
30 Ibid. p. 53
31 Ibid. p. 53
32 Ibid. p. 53
33 Ibid. p. 67
34 Ibid. p. 59
35 Ibid. pps. 462-63
36 Ibid. 278
37 Ibid. 279
38 Ibid.
39 Ibid.
40 Ibid. pps. 282-23
41 Ibid. p. 312
42 Ibid. p. 386
43 Ibid. p. 291
44 Ibid.
45 Ibid. p. 312
46 Ibid. p. 388
47 Ibid. p. 393
48 Ibid. p. 390
49 Ibid. p. 394
50 Ibid. p. 389
51 Ibid. p. 398
52 Ibid. p. 399
53 Ibid. p. 386
54 Jean-Paul Sartre, Existentialism is a Humanism, Yale University Press 2007, p. 22
55 Jean-Paul Sartre, Itinerary of a Thought, New Left Review no. 58 (Nov.-Dec. 1969), p. 45
56 Ibid.
57 Jean-Paul Sartre, Being and Nothingness, Routledge Classics 2002,

	p. 552
58	Jean-Paul Sartre, Existentialism is a Humanism, Yale University Press 2007, p. 38
59	Jean-Paul Sartre, Being and Nothingness, Routledge Classics 2002, p. 494
60	Simone de Beauvoir, The Prime of Life, Penguin Books, 1962, p.22
61	Jean-Paul Sartre, Existentialism is a Humanism, Yale University Press 2007, p. 22
62	Jean-Paul Sartre, No Exit, Vintage Paperback Edition, New York, 1955, pps. 44-45
63	Jean-Paul Sartre, Existentialism is a Humanism, Yale University Press 2007, p. 23
64	Sartre at Seventy – An Interview in New York Review of Books, issue of August 7, 1975
65	Jean-Paul Sartre, Existentialism is a Humanism, Yale University Press 2007, passim
66	Ibid. pps. 23-24
67	Ibid. p. 24
68	Ibid. p. 42
69	Ibid. p. 51

Already published in the same series:

Walther Ziegler
Camus in 60 Minutes
ISBN 9783741227738

Walther Ziegler
Freud in 60 Minutes
ISBN 9783741227707

Walther Ziegler
Hegel in 60 Minutes
ISBN 9783741227677

Walther Ziegler
Heidegger in 60 Minutes
ISBN 9783741227752

Walther Ziegler
Kant in 60 Minutes
ISBN 9783741226373

Walther Ziegler
Marx in 60 Minutes
ISBN 9783741227691

Walther Ziegler
Platon in 60 Minutes
ISBN 9783741227615

Walther Ziegler
Rousseau in 60 Minutes
ISBN 9783741227622

Walther Ziegler
Sartre in 60 Minutes
ISBN 9783741227653

Walther Ziegler
Smith in 60 Minutes
ISBN 9783741227721

Coming soon in the same series:

Walther Ziegler
Adorno in 60 Minutes

Walther Ziegler
Arendt in 60 Minutes

Walther Ziegler
Bacon in 60 Minutes

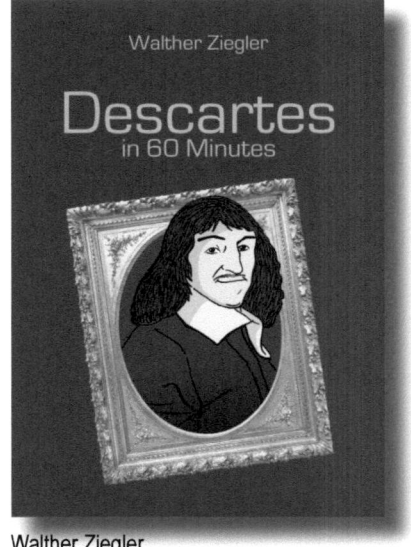

Walther Ziegler
Descartes in 60 Minutes

Walther Ziegler
Foucault in 60 Minutes

Walther Ziegler
Habermas in 60 Minutes

Walther Ziegler
Hobbes in 60 Minutes

Walther Ziegler
Nietzsche in 60 Minutes

Walther Ziegler
Popper in 60 Minutes

Walther Ziegler
Rawls in 60 Minutes

Walther Ziegler
Schopenhauer in 60 Minutes

Walther Ziegler
Wittgenstein in 60 Minutes

The author:

Dr Walther Ziegler is academically trained in the fields of philosophy, history and political science. As a foreign correspondent, reporter and newsroom coordinator for the German TV station ProSieben he has produced films on every continent. His news reports have won several prizes and awards. He has also authored numerous books in the field of philosophy. His many years of experience as a journalist mean that he is able to present the complex ideas of the great philosophers in a way that is both engaging and very clear. Since 2007 he has also been active as a teacher and trainer of young TV journalists in Munich, holding the post of Academic Director at the Media Academy, an institute of higher education that offers film and TV courses at its base directly on the site of the major European film production company Bavaria Film.